AF289942

An Incomplete
Organum for
Documenting
Works of Art

Herstellung und Verlag:
BoD – Books on Demand,
Norderstedt
Gestaltung: Eike Dingler
ISBN: 978-3-7534-3527-5

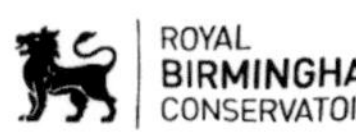

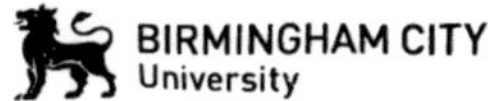

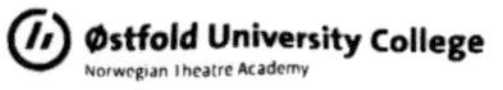

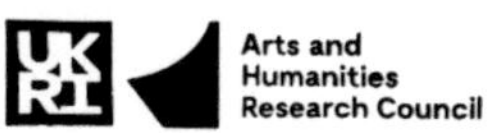

Introduction

How to *document* *music* with non-sonic elements? *Or:* How to document all the performative qualities of a *piece* of music that can't be heard *(like* the sequence of movements within a space, the sweat of the musicians, the heat of the room etc.)? Beginning with this question a group of researchers and dramaturgs from Birmingham (UK), Frankfurt (Germany) and Fredrikstad (Norway) met over the course of 2019 and 2020 to develop initial ideas, questions, rhythms and rhymes.

An Incomplete Organum for Documenting Works of Art is one of the results of the group's discussions, creating twenty-six impulses in the form of hypotheses, questions, considerations and falsities. The *Organum's* purpose is to provoke exchanges about common and uncommon practices for documenting artistic works, and is for artists, scholars, academics and anyone interested. It is divided into three parts: GENERALITIES proposes and tests general definitions of documentation, while STRATEGIES covers pragmatic issues about the role of a documenter or documenters (among other things). MIXED MEDIA then raises questions regarding the conditions of documentation across different genres such as music, film and performance art. None of the twenty-six impulses should be accepted without question; each one is open to debate. An incomplete *Organum* contains incomplete ideas.

My sincere thanks go to the Norwegian Theatre Academy at Høgskolen i Østfold (Anne Berit Løland, Karmenlara Ely and Serge von Arx), Royal Birmingham Conservatoire and the Arts and Humanities Research Council for funding the project and this booklet. My special thanks go to Mira Moschallski, Michael Wolters, Oliver Clark, Paul Norman, Andy Ingamells and Marcus Droß for the discussions in the research group (Andy and Marcus also for their valuable input for this publication), and to Eike Dingler for the graphic design.

Philipp Schulte, November 2020

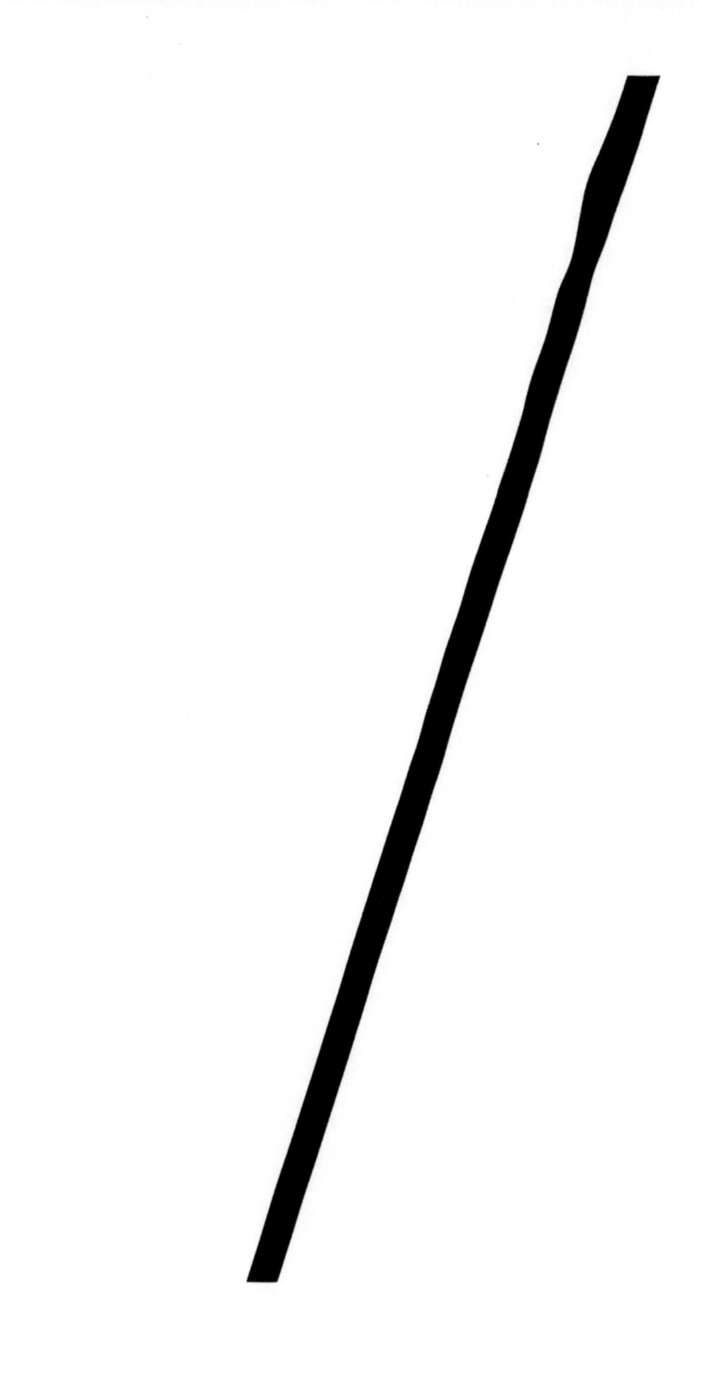

Prologue (1)

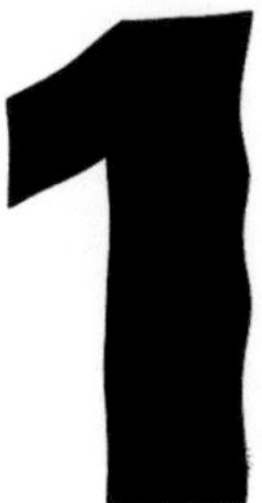

*
Philosopher Hannah
Arendt differs be-
tween action, which
always includes a
notion of beginning
and renewal based
on free decision,
and behaviour, which
is thoroughly con-
ditioned by causal
antecedents, and so
is essentially unfree.
Cp. Hannah Arendt,
*The Human Con-
dition*, 1958.

Every work of art has a public.
Documentation of any work of
art is intended to increase this
public.
So any documentation is – as
any work of art is – an action
that is intended to change the
public.
This also means: Any documentation – as any work of art –
can potentially be considered
political.*

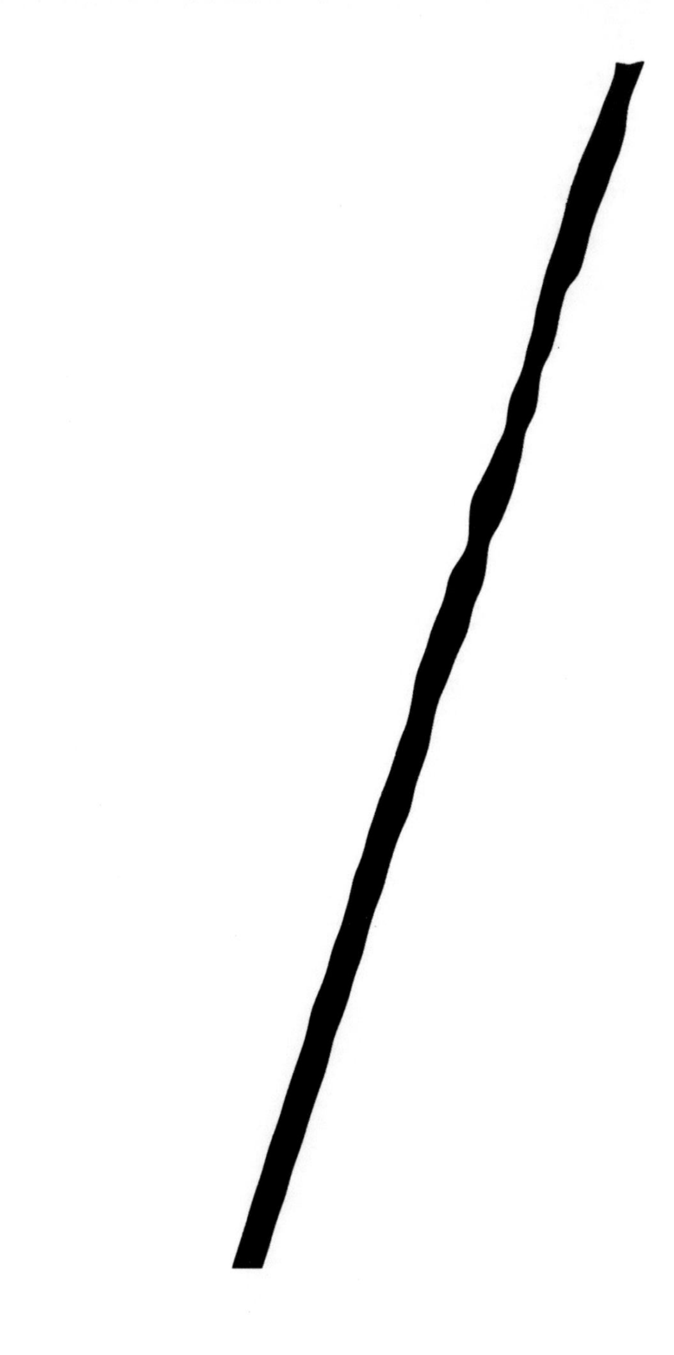

Generalities (2-10)

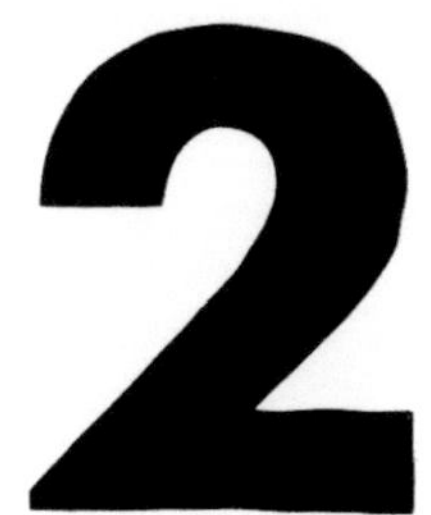

2

The documentation is separate
from the THING that is being
documented (i.e. the 'work').
There is always a loss, or an
addition, or a transformation
which might be aesthetically
interesting
or not
and which might add surplus
value to the work
or not.

What, then, *is* 'good' documentation?

Possible criteria (random list):
– realness
– accuracy
– durability
– readability
– likeability
– distributability
– whatever comes to mind

3

Documentation is a collection of documents. Different kinds of documents can capture different aspects of the work in different ways (and in varying degrees of success). So it's worth considering which kind of documents are collected for which aspects of the work.

4

Documentation has, or will have,
a different audience to that
of the work. So the way a work
is documented and the way the
documentation is presented
depends on the question: FOR
WHOM is this documented?

*Possible audiences for a piece
of documentation (random list):*
– the 'public'
– academics and researchers
– students
– a future audience
– people in another space and
  context
– the artist's mother or grandson
– family, friends and fools
– whatever comes to mind

5

Whether documentation is 'good' or 'bad' can only be measured by its purpose.

******

Blow-up is a 1966 mystery thriller film directed by Michelangelo Antonioni and produced by Carlo Ponti. Its protagonist, a photographer, takes pictures of two lovers in a park. But only after he made enlargements of the black-and-white film the pictures revealed the woman worriedly looking at a third person lurking in the trees with a pistol. In that way he found out more about the photographed situation than he could know at first glance.

So: The way a work is documented and how the documentation
is presented depends on the
question: FOR WHAT PURPOSE
is this documented?

Possible purposes (random list):
– to preserve a work for another
  audience
– to preserve a work for further
  *analysis (the 'Blow-up' effect**)*
– to enable a work to be re-
  enacted, or interpreted
  differently (as in a 'score')
– to publish a work
– to publicise a work
– whatever comes to mind

The PURPOSE of the documentation should always be made
clear at the beginning of the
documentation.

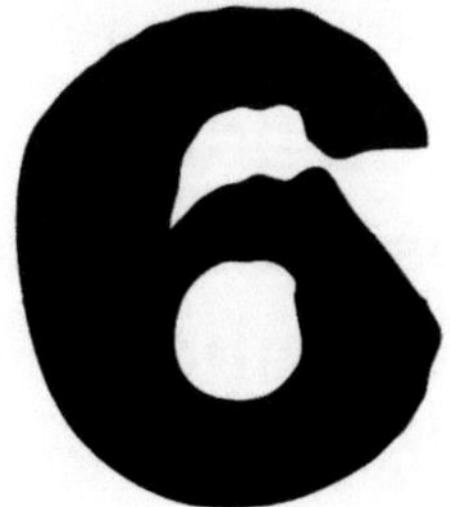

So:

A certain work requires a certain
way of documenting it. There
is not ONE single way. (And it is
definitely not always film).

7

The relationship of documentation to the work is one
of 'fidelity' or 'faithfulness'.

8

Hypothesis:

Good documentation shows that it is documentation (and not the documented work).

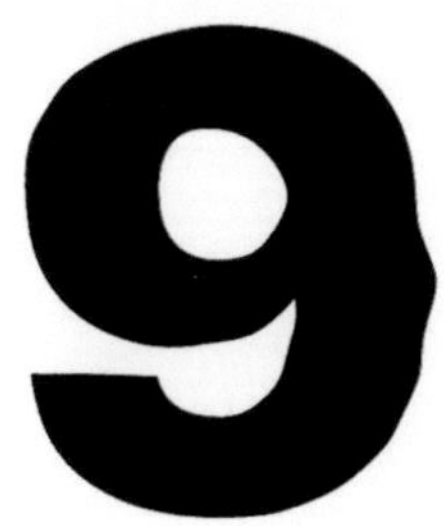

The Paradox of Documentation:
On the one hand good documentation serves the work, and on the other hand it serves its own purpose.

Serving the work means to
preserve as many aspects of the
work as possible, with all the
transformations necessary to
do so (and no more).

Serving the documentation
means to make a careful selection of all the necessary aspects
required to accomplish the
purpose of the documentation
(and no more).

10

Some works are intended to be documented. The documentation might even be part of the work itself.

Some works are not intended
to be documented. In fact,
the nature of some works may
require them to remain eph-
emeral.

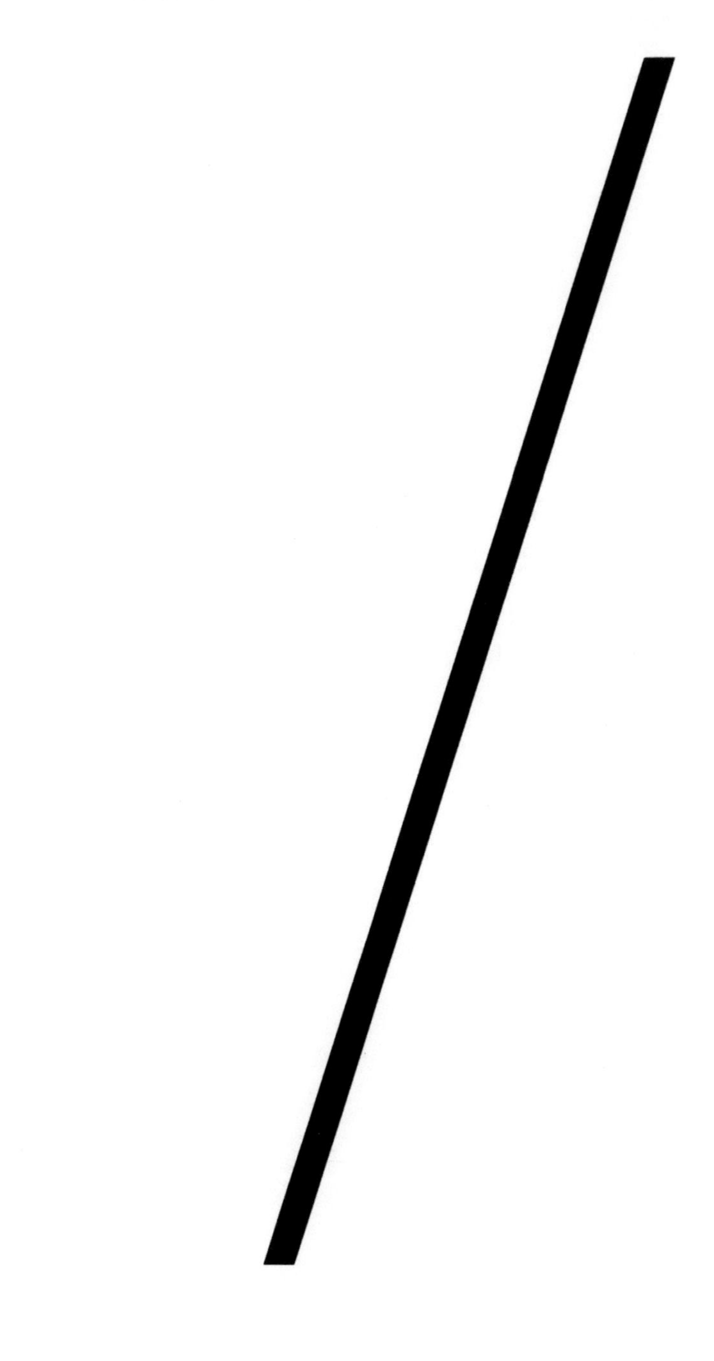

Strategies (11–15)

11

Question:
To what extent is the artistic style of the documenter important for good documentation?

First guess:
It isn't – it's just a disturbance
which distracts from the documented work.

Second guess:
It might be – or at least a certain
aesthetic sensibility towards the
documented work is helpful.

12

From the perspective of the documenter it is not important if the work to be documented is 'good' or 'bad'.
However, a work that is hard to document might be much more interesting for the documenter to document.

13

Every choice a documenter makes is political, especially the choice of works and what aspects of those works are documented and how.

The selection of WHAT is documented *is* a political choice.

The *decisions* about the WAY
in which it is documented are
political choices
but also artistic ones
but also pragmatic ones.

And then there is the question
of what and how it is to be
archived and distributed.

14

Transparency is important.
Whatever is to be documented
and however it is to be done,
the documenter should try
to be as transparent about the
situation in which the piece
was documented as possible.
In that way, the documentation
informs the viewer about the
context of the work as well
as the context of the documentation itself.

15

The presentation of documentation is important. The best possible recording doesn't guarantee an adequate presentation of the documentation.

So:

The quality of an archive also depends on the level of accessibility it provides, as well as on how well the documents within it are (or can be) presented.

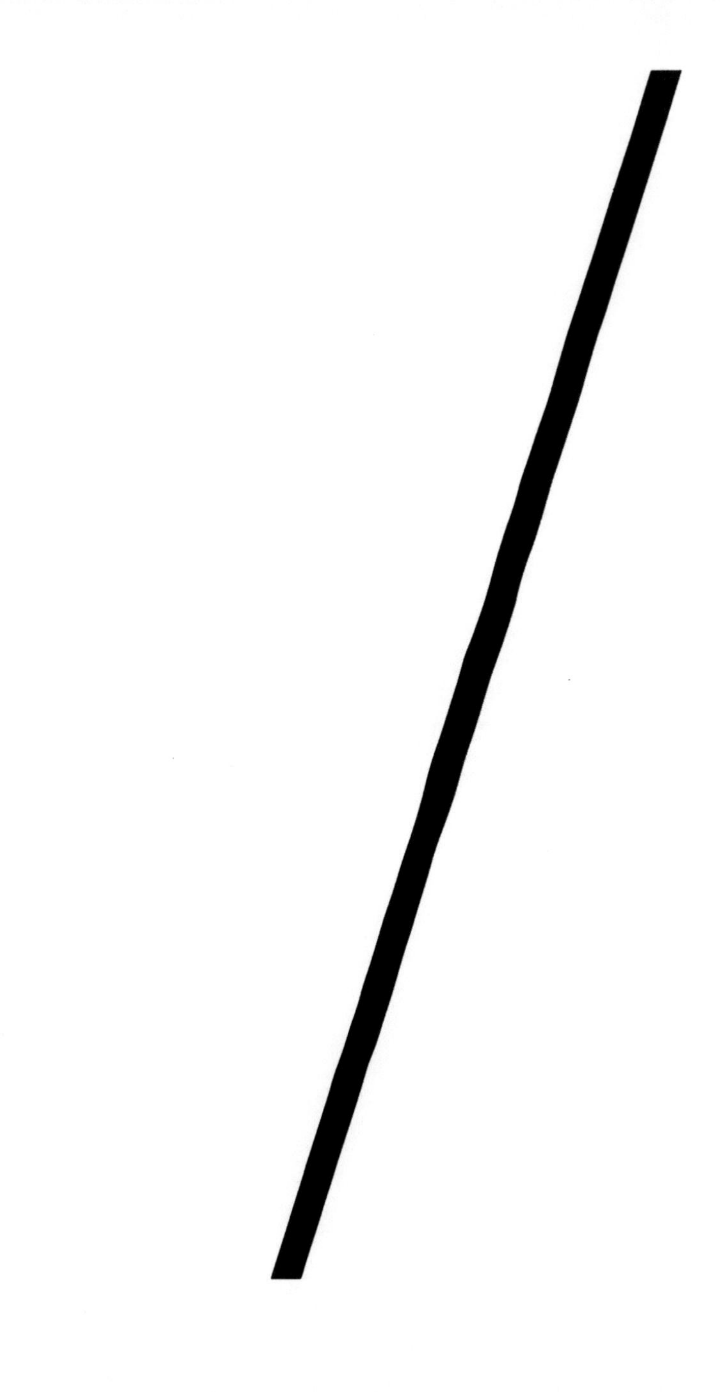

Mixed Media
(16–25)

16

Not every work needs to be documented. If the work itself is already mediatized and distributable (if the work is a digital video clip or a film for example) it might not need to be documented.

On the other hand, a live situation always needs to be documented in order to be preserved
and distributed. It always needs
the transformative, conserving
effects of documentation
to bring it into another context.

17

***

Linguist Noam Chomsky separates competence and performance; he describes 'competence' as an idealized capacity that is located as a psychological or mental property or function and 'performance' as the production of actual utterances. In short, competence involves 'knowing' the language and performance involves 'doing' something with the language. Cp. Noam Chomsky, *Aspects of the Theory of Syntax,* 1965.

If a distinction is made between
the competence of an artistic
utterance and its performance,***
then a documenter must decide
whether to document:
– the competence of a work
   (as in a studio album) or
– the performance of a work
   (as in a live situation)

18

When it comes to video documentation, one contradiction might be between image and movement. How much information about the complete scenery is important? How much (camera) movement is desirable?

Luckily, mixing both is always an option.

19

When it comes to music,
a question:
Is there something like music
without non-sonic elements
at all? (Maybe certain forms of
electronic music?).

Suspicion:
No. Every kind of musical
presentation always happens
in a performative situation.
This situation is either reflected
in the frame of the artwork,
or not. It is either important for
the documentation, or not.

20

It is different if a performance
is done FOR a camera
(or microphone or whatever)
or independent from a camera
(or microphone or whatever).
This doesn't mean a camera
(or a microphone or whatever)
does not document it.

21

Some performances are best documented when they are made for the camera (or microphone or whatever) while pretending they aren't. In this way, the work and its documentation are not mingled.

Some performances are best
documented when processes
of documentation are made
visible. It CAN be important for
good documentation to NOT
hide the way it is documented.
In this way, the work and its
documentation are mingled.

22

Every documenter has to decide how much of the context they want to include in the documentation.

Assumption:
Including impressions of the
context (audience reactions,
camera-person, cameras,
'disturbances' etc.) helps
the viewer of the documentation to recreate the live
situation of the work and learn
something about its surround-
ings and effects.

23

A *documenter* of time-based
works (like *performances*)
always has to decide when
to start *documenting* and when
to finish documenting. Does
the documentation start when
the performance starts and
finish when it finishes? Or are
the moments before the
beginning and after the ending
included?

24

Question:

Since there is no such thing as
a performance without context,
why should there be documentation that erases context?

25

When it comes to score-based
artworks, another question:

Does a score constitute documentation of the concept(s)
and idea(s) that formed a work?

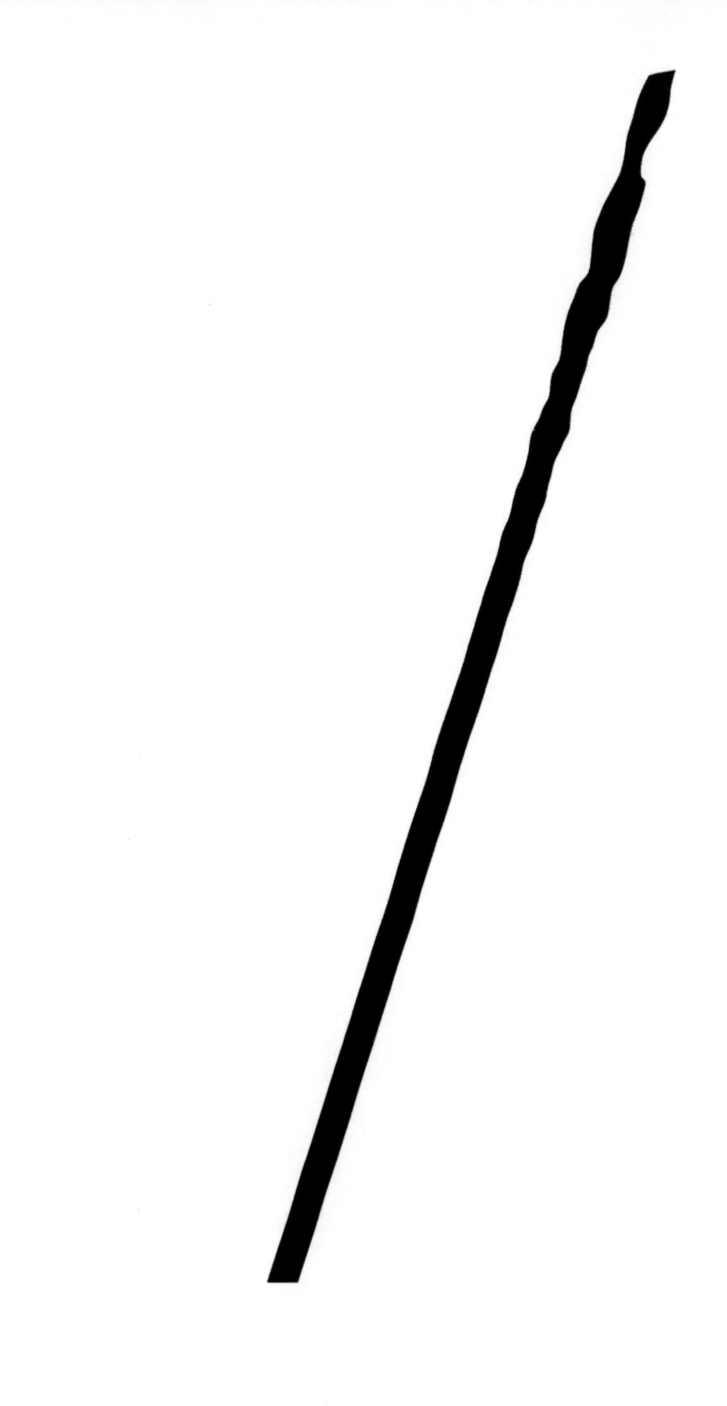

Epilogue
(26)

26

Finally, when *it* comes to the question of documenting music *with* non-sonic elements, it is important to consider that every single musical performance always consists of a combination of sonic and non-sonic elements. Documenting only the sonic elements, either because of conventional thinking
or because we know it works
or because we developed good technologies to do that or because it might be complicated to think about how to document non-sonic elements
or just because we consider the non-sonic elements as less important, is thoughtless and feeble. Documentation and its technologies should always serve the work of art and not the other way around.

26

Finally, when it comes to the question of documenting music with non-sonic elements, it is important to consider that every single musical performance always consists of a combination of sonic and non-sonic elements. Documenting only the sonic elements, either because of conventional thinking or because we know it works or because we developed good technologies to do that or because it might be complicated to think about how to document non-sonic elements or just because we consider the non-sonic elements as less important, is thoughtless and feeble. Documentation and its technologies should always serve the work of art and not the other way around.

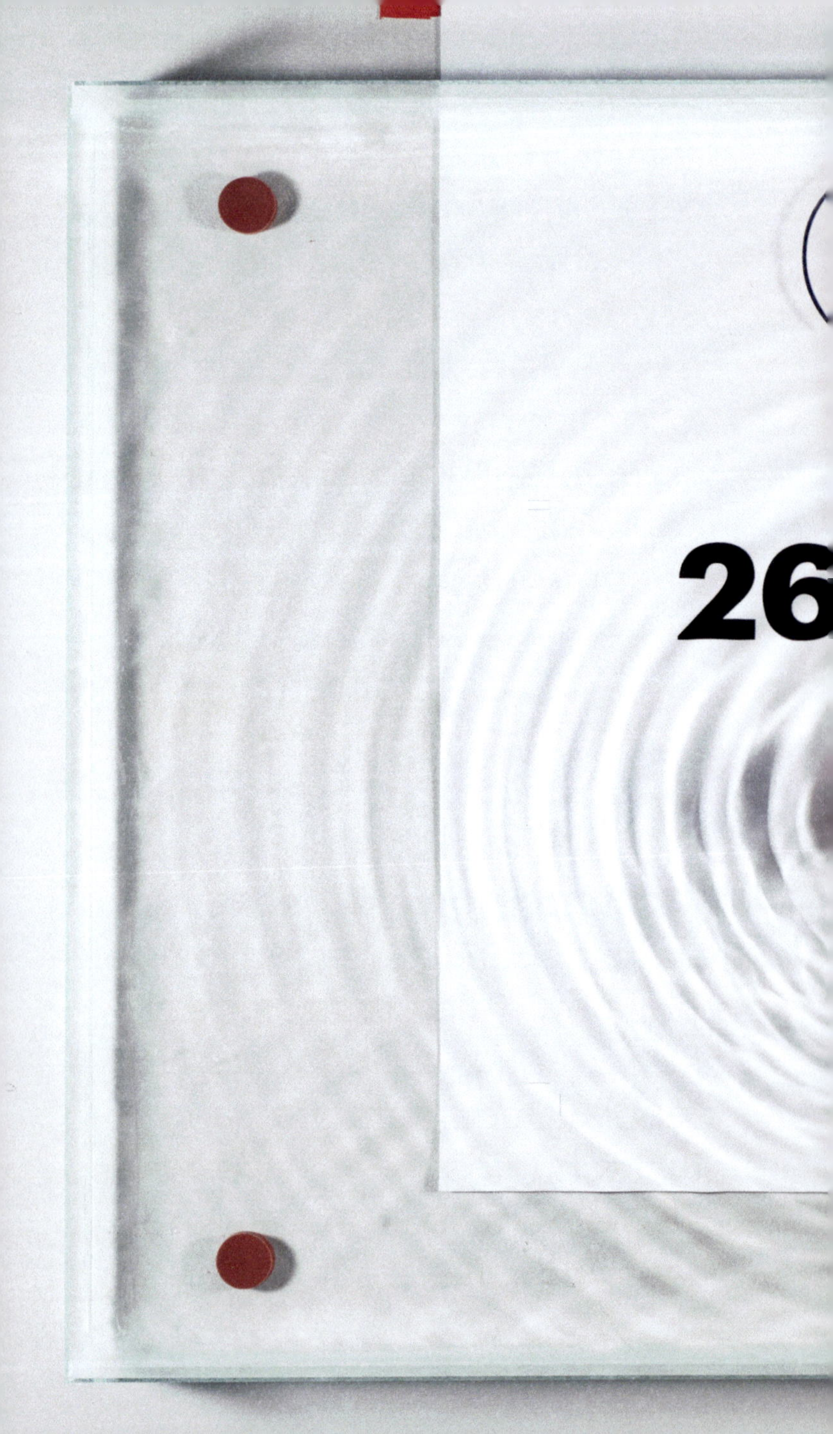

Finally, when it comes to the question of documenting music with non-sonic elements, it is important to consider that every single musical performance always consists of a combination of sonic and non-sonic elements. Documenting only the sonic elements, either because of conventional thinking or because we know it works or because we developed good technologies to do that or because it might be complicated to think about how to document non-sonic elements or just because we consider the non-sonic elements as less important, is thoughtless and feeble. Documentation and its technologies should always serve the work of art and not the other way around.

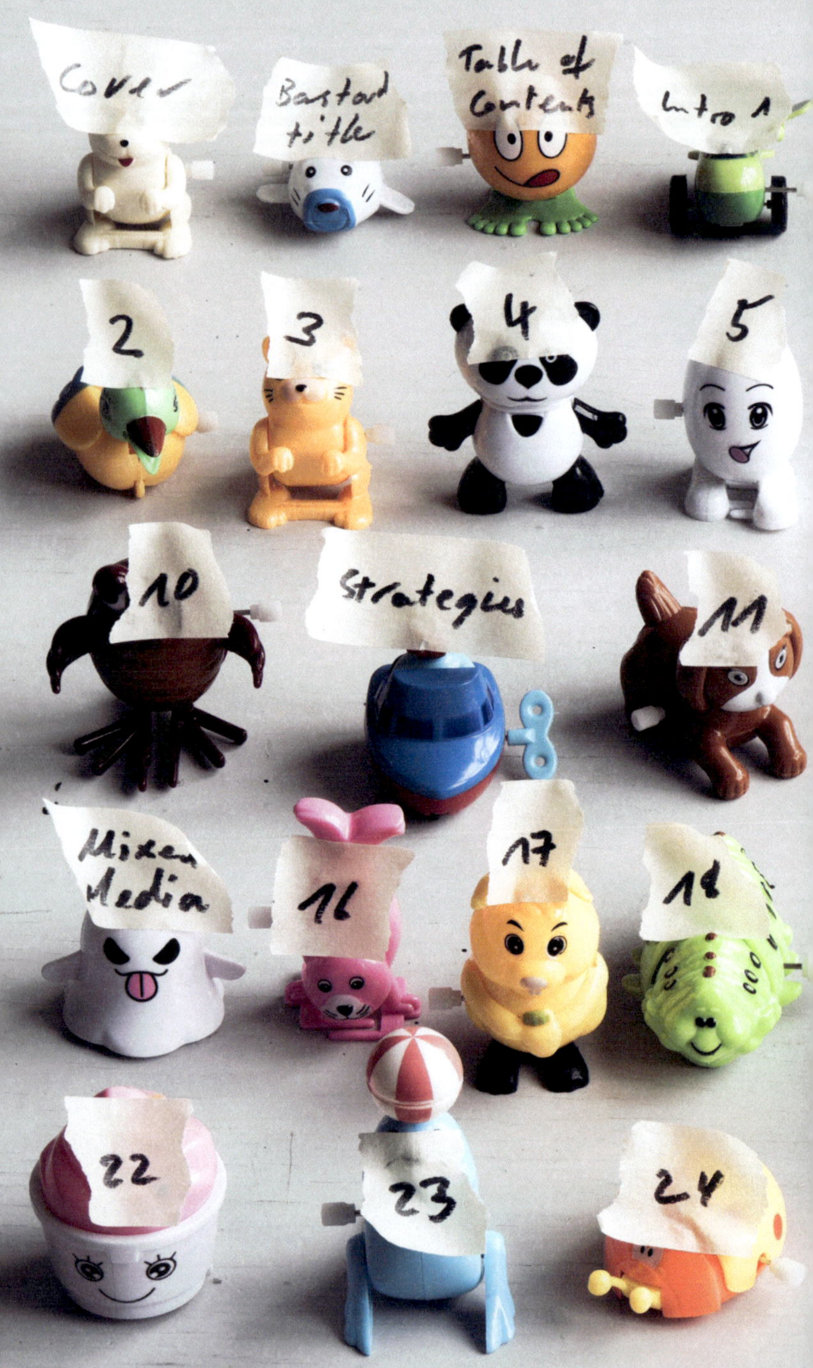

Cover
Bastard title
Table of Contents
Intro 1
2
3
4
5
10
Strategies
11
Mixed Media
16
17
18
22
23
24

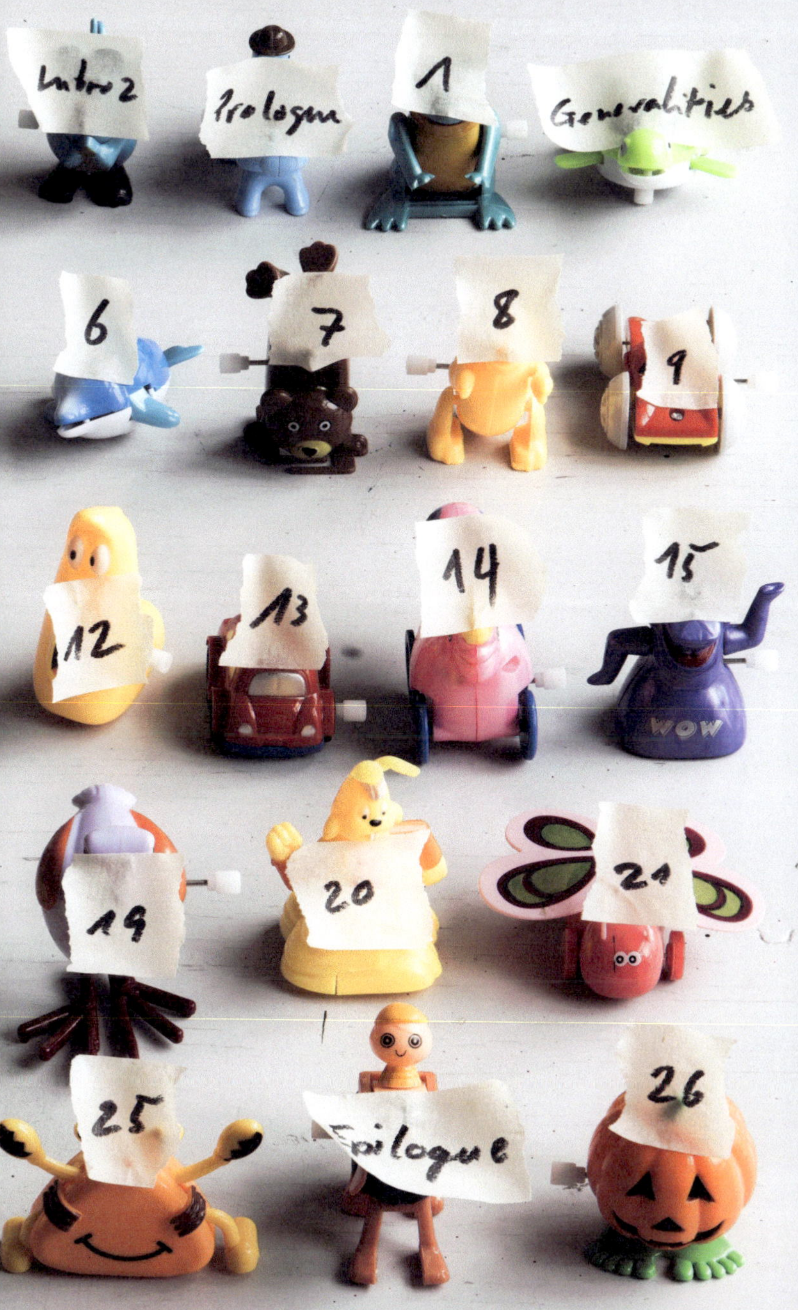

Intro 2
Prologue
1
Generalities
6
7
8
9
12
13
14
15
19
20
21
25
Epilogue
26
WOW